AXIS

OF

BEGINNING

JOSEPH N. PAQUETTE

Axis of Beginning
Copyright © 2022 Joseph N. Paquette

Produced and printed by Stillwater River Publications.
All rights reserved. Written and produced in the
United States of America. This book may not be reproduced
or sold in any form without the expressed, written
permission of the author and publisher.

Visit our website at
www.StillwaterPress.com
for more information.

First Stillwater River Publications Edition

ISBN: 978-1-955123-97-6

Library of Congress Control Number: 2022905521

1 2 3 4 5 6 7 8 9 10
Written by Joseph N. Paquette
Cover design by Joseph N. Paquette
Cover & author portrait photography by Donna M. St.Pierre
https://www.facebook.com/DonnaMarieStPierre
https://www.flickr.com/thetraveledpath
Published by Stillwater River Publications,
Pawtucket, RI, USA.

Publisher's Cataloging-In-Publication Data
(Prepared by The Donohue Group, Inc.)

Names: Paquette, Joseph N., author.
Title: Axis of Beginning / Joseph N. Paquette.
Description: First Stillwater River Publications edition. |
Pawtucket, RI, USA : Stillwater River Publications, [2022]
Identifiers: ISBN 9781955123976
Subjects: LCSH: Families--Religious life--Drama. |
Christianity and atheism--Drama. |
Intelligent design (Teleology)--Drama. |
Evolution (Biology)--Drama.
Classification: LCC PS3616.A68 A95 2022 |
DDC 812/.6--dc23

AXIS OF BEGINNING

CONTENTS

AUTHOR'S NOTE

I was raised as a Christian. The idea of an all-powerful being taking care of the universe's business while being aware of us is worthy of attention. So, when I began reading the Bible in my late teens, I accepted the Gospels as historical records about real people. However, what the Genesis narrative tells us of the beginning does not align with what science teaches. So, as a result, I accepted the story of creation on faith.

Later, as an adult, I read an article in a popular science magazine about the Wilkinson Microwave Anisotropy Probe (WMAP) and how its data reveals that our earth and solar system may be cosmically aligned. Then came the Planck satellite confirming the WMAP data. Could this be evidence that the book of Genesis is based on historical events? Perhaps, but unfortunately, I am not a scientist and could only understand about 1 percent of the science. Nevertheless, according to cosmologists, one thing is evident: the alignments somehow exist! Moreover, because the data does not fit the Standard Model of Cosmology, scientists dubbed it the Axis of Evil. But, according to Genesis, the alignments would be the Axis of Beginning and the inspiration for writing this story.

PRODUCTION NOTES

CHARACTERS

RAYMOND — Fred's brother. Army jacket, T-shirts, jeans, and work boots.

FRED — Elizabeth's husband. Blue suit with striped ties.

ELIZABETH — Fred's wife. Vibrant, colorful dresses.

CHRISTINE — Elizabeth's cousin. Fashionable pantsuits and blouses.

DUDE — Barking Dog *(Voice Over)*.

Characters are 30ish or 40ish years old. Raymond and Christine are at least five years younger than Fred and Elizabeth.

SCENE/STAGE

The action takes place in the family room of Elizabeth and Fred's Victorian home in Brookline, Massachusetts.

Slightly right of center stage facing each other are two armchairs, each with a side-end table with books and a shaded lamp. A little left of center stage is a sofa with a coffee table. Upstage right is an opening leading off stage to a hallway, the front door, and a room where Dude resides. Upstage is a serving table with dinnerware. Upstage left is a bookcase with books and a globe. All the above, and more or less at the set designer's discretion.

ACT ONE

The present. An afternoon and evening in April.

ACT TWO

Three months later, an afternoon in July and the following evening.

NOTES

The ellipses (. . .) show hesitation or trailing off of dialogue.

The Emdash (--) indicates cutting off with simultaneous dialogue.

(V.O.) Voice Over. Character as narrator.

(O.S.) Off-stage. The character speaks off-stage before entering.

AXIS OF BEGINNING

ACT I

A dark stage.

RAYMOND *(V.O.)*
"In the beginning was the Word, and the Word was with God, and the Word was God. The same was in the beginning with God. All things were made by Him, and without Him was not anything made that was made."

(The lights rise on the living room. Elizabeth is adjusting her husband's tie.)

ELIZABETH
Fred. Would you please hold still?

FRED
It was fine before we began fussing.

ELIZABETH
(She moves away.)
Now it's better.

(Fred becomes centered on pacing.)

FRED
He should be here by now.

ELIZABETH
Relax. He's your brother, not my mother.

                    FRED
Elizabeth. Please do not dismiss my concern.

                  ELIZABETH
                  (Upbeat.)
Let's play "name that quote."

                    FRED
Not interested . . .

                  ELIZABETH
Charades?

                    FRED
Just the two of us?
     (He crosses to the serving table.)
We should have insisted on picking him
up.

                  ELIZABETH
He doesn't need us to fuss over him.

                    FRED
          (He pours a drink.)
Would you like a seltzer?

                  ELIZABETH
You decide; you know better.

     *(Fred turns, studies his wife for a
     moment.)*

> FRED

Is that a new dress?

> ELIZABETH

Yes, do you like it?

> FRED

Did you buy it because of Raymond's visit?

> ELIZABETH
> *(She sits on the sofa.)*

Why did you assume I bought it because of you?

> FRED

Do we need sarcasm?

> ELIZABETH

Would you prefer I humor you, dear?

> FRED

You know Raymond is always punctual.

> ELIZABETH

"Be anxious for nothing . . ."

> FRED
> *(Puzzled.)*

Is that a quote I am supposed to recognize?

                    ELIZABETH
It's from the Bible.

                      FRED
Elizabeth, why are you quoting from the
Bible?

                    ELIZABETH
It's a popular book.

                      FRED
You are confronting me to distract me--

                    ELIZABETH
Conjecture . . .

                      FRED
Before I argue the premise, "Be anxious
for nothing," I would need to understand
the statement in its written context.
Sadly for you, there is not enough inter-
est on my behalf to pursue such a thought
experiment.

                    ELIZABETH
Humor me . . .

        (A car horn sounds and Dude barks.)

                      FRED
That must be Raymond.

*(Fred exits and Elizabeth stands.
The doorbell chimes and Dude barks
again.)*

FRED *(O.S.)*
Dude, it is Uncle Raymond.

(We hear the front door opening.)

RAYMOND *(O.S.)*
(Excitedly, loud.)
Freddy . . . !

FRED *(O.S.)*
Raymond, come in, come in!

RAYMOND *(O.S.)*
(Over-the-top.)
You look great!

FRED *(O.S.)*
As you . . . Who is that? A friend?

RAYMOND *(O.S.)*
Uber.

(We hear the front door closing.)

RAYMOND *(O.S.)*
Hey, Dude, how are you doing, old buddy?
Freddy, let him out.

FRED *(O.S.)*
Unfortunately, we are entering his spring
shedding cycle. Fortunately, the big boy
is going in for a cut tomorrow.

>   *(A moment later, the brothers*
>   *enter. Raymond drops his duffle bag*
>   *and crosses to Elizabeth. They*
>   *hug.)*

RAYMOND
Liz, it's so good to see you.

ELIZABETH
Raymond, we're delighted you're finally
here . . .
>   *(She fusses up his hair.)*
. . . and you need a haircut.

RAYMOND
That's a stunning dress. And I love the
shoes.

ELIZABETH
Thank you. I bought them just for this
occasion.

>   *(From the duffle bag, Raymond removes*
>   *two small boxes.)*

RAYMOND
Here; for you, and one for you.

(Elizabeth opens her gift: a necklace.)

ELIZABETH
It's lovely.

*(She places the necklace on her
neck and Fred fastens the clasp.)*

FRED
Yes, it goes perfectly with your new
dress, dear.

RAYMOND
One of my students, Karen, made it.

FRED
A very talented young lady.

ELIZABETH
Thank you, and tell Karen I love it.

*(Fred opens his gift, removes the
object.)*

FRED
(Perplexed.)
Raymond . . . A trilobite fossil--?

ELIZABETH
Fred, it's beautiful! Almost translucent.
Is it real?

                    RAYMOND
I carved it out of quartz.

                     FRED
It is a unique gift. Superb. Very sophisticated design, a credit to your talent.
It must have taken you a long time to
have achieved such detail.

                    RAYMOND
It didn't take as long as you think.

                     FRED
Thank you, Raymond.

                    RAYMOND
Is Chris coming?

                   ELIZABETH
Yes, hopefully Christine will be here
shortly.

                    RAYMOND
I'd like to freshen up.

                   ELIZABETH
Your room's ready, and I laid out fresh
linen.

     (Raymond swings the duffle bag over
     his shoulder and exits. Dude Barks.
     Fred holds the carving above his
     head and he and Elizabeth examine

the artifact as lights fade out to black.)

ELIZABETH *(V.O.)*
"Study to show yourself approved to God, a workman that need not be ashamed, rightly dividing the word of truth."

(The doorbell chimes; Dude barks. Lights rise on the vacant room.)

ELIZABETH *(O.S.)*
Hush boy. Behave. Lie down.

(We hear the front door opening.)

ELIZABETH *(O.S.)*
You're late.

CHRISTINE *(O.S.)*
Traffic is terrible.

ELIZABETH *(O.S.)*
Then you should know by now to leave home sooner.

CHRISTINE *(O.S.)*
Hello, Dude . . .

(We hear the front door closing.)

ELIZABETH *(O.S.)*
Let me take your coat.

                    CHRISTINE *(O.S.)*
Let the poor boy out.

                    ELIZABETH *(O.S.)*
And listen to you complain about how he's
shedding all over? Besides, Fred vacuumed
this morning.

     (They enter, crossing to the serv-
     ing table.)

                    CHRISTINE
Is Ray here?

                    ELIZABETH
Yes, he and Fred are in the garage.

          (Elizabeth pours coffee.)

                    CHRISTINE
Did he ask about me?

                    ELIZABETH
          (She hands Christine the cup.)
He knows you were coming.

                    CHRISTINE
How does he look?

                    ELIZABETH
He's beginning to look like Dude.

CHRISTINE

What . . . look like Dude?

ELIZABETH

He needs a haircut.

CHRISTINE

It must be at least three years since
we've seen each other. Or is it four?

ELIZABETH

Three and a half, and please, don't overwhelm the conversation. You know today is
about the boys.

CHRISTINE
(Calling out.)

"Overwhelm the conversation--?"

ELIZABETH

Hush, they'll hear you . . .

FRED (O.S.)

Yes, Raymond, you always had a healthy
imagination.

RAYMOND (O.S.)

Freddy, please, for once, take me seri-
ously--

FRED (O.S.)

Do you take me for a fool?

                    RAYMOND *(O.S.)*
The foolish celebrate life as if it will
go on forever with no judgment at the end.

                    FRED *(O.S.)*
I do not need the crutch of religion to
validate my existence. A person who uses
a deity as a crutch is a fool. Christian
blind faith leads us back to the Dark
Ages.

          (Fred and Raymond enter.)

                    RAYMOND
Faith is never blind . . .
                    (cheerfully)
Chris . . .

                    CHRISTINE
Ray, you're a Christian? I mean, you look
well. Not that you couldn't be a Christian
. . . Please, jump in anytime, so I'm not
standing here like a babbling idiot.

     *(Raymond removes tickets from his
      pocket and hands them to Christine.)*

                    RAYMOND
Here, for you and Liz.

                    CHRISTINE
Journey! Lizzy, the band *Journey*, we were
saying we should go.

                    ELIZABETH
Fred, did you have a part in this?

                      FRED
Guilty.

                   CHRISTINE
Ray, Fred, thank you both for thinking of
me.

     (Raymond and Christine cross to the
     sofa, Fred and Elizabeth sit in the
     armchairs.)

                    RAYMOND
So, Chris, what's new . . . ?

                   CHRISTINE
Still teaching yoga, and I left Davenport
and secured a position at Steward Elementary.

                    RAYMOND
Yes, I heard . . .

                   CHRISTINE
It's a substantial pay cut, but I was sick
and tired of deadlines. It's less stress-
ful teaching third graders. That is, once
you show them who's the boss. And you?

                    RAYMOND
Still at the School of Visual Arts.

ELIZABETH
Raymond was offered a chair position.

CHRISTINE
That sounds like an excellent opportunity.

RAYMOND
Yes, but unfortunately, there is a little
more involved with the position, which
will compromise my time in the classroom—

FRED
(He stands.)
Yes, yes, Raymond! We all have to make
compromises for our careers, but to con-
clude our conversation, the Bible is an
invention of early man's superstitions.
(He sits.)
Ernst Haeckel said, "Science has to pluck
the blessed fruits from the tree of
knowledge, unconcerned whether these con-
quests trench upon the poetical imagin-
ings of faith or not."

RAYMOND
C.S. Lewis stated, "Men became scientific
because they expected law in nature, and
they expected law in nature because they
believed in a lawgiver."

ELIZABETH

As much as this subject is fascinating, I
imagine it would be best if you and Raymond discussed this later.

FRED

Elizabeth, let me finish.
(He stands.)
What I am asking is, do religious doc-
trines inspire ignorance? Can you sepa-
rate faith from short-sightedness?

RAYMOND

In his book, *The Ultimate Proof of Creation*, Jason Lisle wrote, I'll paraphrase: Creationists and evolutionists
have different worldviews and interpret
the same evidence differently. Similarly,
many Christians have different theological
views as well.

ELIZABETH

Perhaps this is the time to agree to disagree.

FRED

(He sits.)
Yes, Raymond. Too much time has elapsed
between us to be arguing, so for the sake
of argument . . .

RAYMOND
Freddy, I have no intention of agreeing
with you concerning God's word.

(Elizabeth and Christine are sur-
prised at Raymond. Fred, annoyed,
stands and crosses to his brother.)

FRED
(Pointedly.)
Faith in deities is the path of least
resistance for the weak, and compensates
with answers that gratify emotions by
alleviating fears.

RAYMOND
"Without faith, it is impossible to
please him, for he who comes to God must
believe that he is . . ."

FRED
(He laughs, crosses back)
Raymond . . . Raymond, for goodness'
sake, please do not end up like one of
those . . . those . . .
(He sits.)
Religious fanatics, spewing out memorized
Bible verses at inappropriate times . . .

ELIZABETH
(She stands.)
Takeout from Tony's Pizza. Anchovies,
anyone?

CHRISTINE

I'm game . . .

FRED

"That which can be asserted without evidence can be dismissed without evidence."

RAYMOND

Christopher Hitchens--

ELIZABETH

Anyone up for a game of charades?

FRED

Sam Harris said faith is the license religious people give to keep believing when reason fails.

ELIZABETH

Fred, please. Arguing isn't the way toward reconciliation.

CHRISTINE

As someone who isn't invested in religion, I'm curious. Ray, what motivated you to become a Christian?

RAYMOND

I'll answer by asking: do you know where you're going to spend eternity--?

FRED

Yes, at Elm Grove Cemetery.

CHRISTINE
Sometimes, I wake in the middle of the
night, anxious by the thought of dying.
I'm unsure if it is the process or what
exists after that terrifies me the most.

ELIZABETH
(She sits.)
Could it be the movies you watch before
going to bed?

RAYMOND
I would be less concerned about the process and more concerned about having my
name written in the Lamb's Book of Life.

FRED
Deities do not exist, but must exist, if
only for control of the populous. And for
the record, I am an advocate of Darwinism
and New Atheism.

RAYMOND
What if, after death, there is *something*
rather than *nothing?*

FRED
Then I may have to admit you were right,
but until then. . .

RAYMOND
Freddy, have you read the Bible?

FRED

Raymond, you are too late in the day and early in the week to convince me that the Bible is anything more than non-scientific.

RAYMOND

The Bible describes scientific phenomena which were unavailable when God inspired the books to be written.

FRED

The Bible is made up of myths written by goat herders; it is not a collection of scientific papers.

RAYMOND

In Proverbs, we're asked to consider the ant who stores *her* food in the summer and gathers *her* food in the harvest. How did goat herders know that worker ants are all girl ants?

FRED

Poetic license. In the primitive, ancient, sexist world of goat herders, the female was associated with foraging and nurturing.

RAYMOND

Freddy, can you assess a book you never read? The word is designed to open our hearts to the truth.

                    FRED
"What is truth?"

                  ELIZABETH
Now *you're* quoting the Bible, dear.

                    FRED
I have participated in discussions with
theists, agnostics, atheists, and Torah
scholars, who agree that we should not
take most Biblical scriptures literally.

                  ELIZABETH
My husband is serious. He never uses the
term "literally" liberally.

                  RAYMOND
The Bible was written over a span of fif-
teen hundred years, by forty different
authors, in three languages, on three
different continents.
        (He stands, crossing to Fred.)
Some authors were unaware of what was
written before or what came after.
Regardless, they formed sixty-six books
of a single, God-inspired, integrated
message: His perfect plan for salvation.

                    FRED
Yes, the Bible has been rewritten numer-
ous times, with various interpretations
due to copyright laws.
        (He laughs.)

A telephone, story-carousel game.

                    RAYMOND
"The words of the Lord are pure words, as
silver tried in a furnace of earth, puri-
fied seven times."
          (He crosses back and sits.)
I would imagine even atheists would be
curious about what's contained in its
ancient volumes.

     (Fred stands, crossing to Raymond.)

                     FRED
Was it curiosity that led you to become
ensnared by its propaganda? That book
does not recognize science, nor does science depend on the language of that book.

                    RAYMOND
"Ask the beasts, and they will teach you,
and the birds of the air will tell you,
speak to the earth, and it will show you,
and the fish of the sea will explain to
you that every living thing is in His
hand and the breath of all mankind."

                   CHRISTINE
Ray, that was beautiful.

                     FRED
Yes, fine poetry. Learned by heart. And
non-scientific.

(The lights go out.)

CHRISTINE *(V.O.)*
"Behold what manner of love the Father
has bestowed on us, that we should be
called children of God! Therefore the
world does not know us because it did not
know Him."

(Lights rise on Fred and Raymond,
seated in armchairs. Raymond is
scrolling on his phone.)

FRED
The Medieval Crusades were bloody, polit-
ical-military enterprises conducted under
the petition to recover the Holy Land.
The Spanish Papal Inquisition investi-
gated, tortured, and murdered hundreds of
thousands who were suspected of insin-
cerity toward the faith. The Salem witch
trials. An endless list of good intentions.

RAYMOND
John Lennox establishes a powerful image
between good and evil when he writes:
(He reads from his phone.)
"I've learned to distinguish between the
greatness of God and the inexcusable
evil that has been done by those professing His name . . . After all, if I
failed to distinguish between the genius

of Einstein and the abuse of his science
to create weapons of mass destruction, I
might be tempted to say science is not
great, and technology poisons everything."

                    FRED
Understanding right from wrong is a
by-product of evolution. Millions of
years of ancestral behavior, anticipating
consequences for the survival of the col-
lective.

      (Throughout the following, Eliz-
      abeth enters with a tray of hors
      d'oeuvres, crossing to the serving
      table.)

                   RAYMOND
Without God, there is no true morality or
justice.

                    FRED
Then your position is established: only
the Judeo-Christian God may account for
morality, and the rest of us are deluded?

      (Fred stands, crossing to his wife.)

                    FRED
I consider myself an ethical and moral
man without the need for religion.

                    RAYMOND
Freddy, what if being made, formed, and
created in God's image and likeness is
what establishes morality in every indi-
vidual?
                    (He pauses.)
That would define eternal truths, but not
interfere with our free will to operate
the ability to be morally subjective.

                      FRED
Through evolution, I agree that morality
is subjective, intuitive to each individ-
ual.

        *(Elizabeth feeds her husband an
        hors d'oeuvre.)*

                    RAYMOND
The world needed laws, then a Savior to
fulfill the law.

                      FRED
Hmm . . . Very good . . .

                   ELIZABETH
            (She crosses to Raymond.)
"The arc of the moral universe is long,
but it bends toward justice."

                      FRED
               (Enthusiastically.)
Martin Luther King, Jr.

*(She offers Raymond an hors d'oeu-
vre. He takes one.)*

RAYMOND

Thank you.

(Elizabeth exits.)

FRED

Transcendence is a misleading misconcep-
tion.

(Raymond stands, crossing to Fred.)

RAYMOND

The fall of humanity was catastrophic.
Flies in the ointment that contaminated
God's creation led to death.

FRED

Yes, once upon a time, a certain couple
ate a piece of forbidden produce, prompt-
ing the world to fall into chaos.
                    (He pauses.)
A statement attributed to Epicurus: Is
God willing to prevent evil but unable?
Or is He able but unwilling? Whence,
then, is evil?

RAYMOND

"The heaven, even the heavens, are the
Lord's, but the earth He has given to the
children of men." God gave us the title

deed to this planet, and we gave it away and allowed evil into the world. "Whence, then, is evil?"

                    FRED
During the Second World War, six million Jewish people were killed in the Holo-caust.
          (He folds his arms.)
Why does God allow evil to exist?

                  RAYMOND
I don't know.

                    FRED
Maybe because there is no God.

                  RAYMOND
Perhaps giving away the title deed was even more severe than we are distracted to accept.
            (He pauses.)
So, then we wonder why evil exists and blame God. But, unfortunately, this mind-set has become business as usual.

                    FRED
So this all-powerful and all-knowing deity endows us with authority over this planet, and we give it away, so He pun-ishes us. Then we give Him a free pass?
            (He pauses.)
That sounds like a setup to me.

RAYMOND

We can't blame God for what men advance;
humanity is easily led and selfishly cor-
rupt. Even Jesus fought against the religious leaders of His time.

FRED

Apparently, Epicurus was correct.

RAYMOND

C.S. Lewis expressed it best when he
wrote, "Free will, though it makes evil
possible, is also the only thing that
makes possible any love or goodness or
joy worth having."
                    (He pauses.)
Albert Einstein said, "God did not create
evil. Just as darkness is the absence of
light, evil is the absence of God."

FRED

As I understand, Einstein was an atheist.

RAYMOND

Truly, God works in mysterious ways.

FRED

"A puppet is free as long as he loves his
strings."

RAYMOND

Sam Harris, again?

(A moment passes.)

FRED

I have a colleague whose nine-year-old daughter, Katlyn, has leukemia. Raymond, what of Katlyn?

RAYMOND

I don't know. "For my thoughts are not your thoughts, neither are your ways my ways, says the Lord."

FRED

So God spins His great roulette wheel, and wherever the roulette pill falls, a curse for some, a blessing for others, becomes our fate?

RAYMOND

Because of free will, what part we play in God's sovereign, eternal plan, for better or worse, I believe, is entirely up to us. We can either sow to the flesh or sow to the spirit.
(Pointedly.)
"Be not deceived; God is not mocked: for whatsoever a man sows, that shall he also reap."

FRED
(Pointedly.)
And what did little Katlyn sow to reap such a disease?

                    RAYMOND
I . . . I'm sorry, that was very insensitive. Not what I meant. I wasn't implying
that Katlyn or her parents brought this
on.

                    FRED
Yes, let us blame your overzealous, heed-
less manner of being caught up in a Biblical textbook moment.

                    RAYMOND
An illness is frightening and devastat-
ing for a family without faith. Are they
Christians?

                    FRED
I do not know. Fortunately, Katlyn is in
remission.

                    RAYMOND
Thank God.

                    FRED
Yes, they were lucky.

                (A pause.)

                    RAYMOND
God is not removed from human suffering.
God's Son was a man and was punished for
our sins. Beaten beyond recognition.
Humiliated and hung on a tree for our

salvation. ". . . And by His stripes, we are healed."
(He sits.)
I love what J. R. R. Tolkien wrote: "The birth, death, and resurrection of Jesus means that one day everything sad will come untrue."

FRED

Richard Dawkins expresses it well when he writes:
(He sits.)
"We are all atheists about most of the gods that humanity has ever believed in. Some of us just go one god further."

RAYMOND

God formed man from dust and breathed the breath of life, Consciousness, into him, and man became a living being, made in His image and likeness, with the potential to be moral and with a free will to accept or reject His salvation.
(He considers.)
What rewards would there be in forcing Elizabeth to love you?

FRED

How insulting! Force my wife to love me?

RAYMOND

And would her unwillingness to freely love you be worthy of dying over?

FRED

Worthy of dying over . . . ?

RAYMOND

"But God demonstrates His love toward
us, in that while we were still sinners,
Christ died for us."

FRED
    (He stands, crossing to Raymond.)
Raymond, Raymond, wishful thinking has
invariably misled you. Materialism
explains the universe quite well without
a God hypothesis leading the way.

RAYMOND
    (He stands.)
Men like Adolf Hitler, Joseph Stalin, Mao
Tse-tung, and other tyrants, at their discretion, tortured and murdered. Evolution will never judge these men for their
crimes. How can materialism establish laws
of morality without first the ability to
discern between good and evil? Sin brought
death, and science calls it "evolution."

(The lights go out.)

RAYMOND *(V.O.)*
"And God said, Let Us make man in Our
image, according to Our Likeness; let
them have dominion over the fish of the
sea, over the birds of the air, and over

the cattle, over all the earth and over every creeping thing that creeps on the earth."

(*The lights rise on Fred, sitting on the sofa, flipping pages of a book. Raymond is seated in an arm-chair.*)

FRED

Charles Darwin's book was published on November 24, 1859. A monumental master-piece of scientific literature that has transformed how we observe the natural world.
(*He clears his throat, reads.*)
On the Origin of Species by Means of Nat-ural Selection or the Preservation of Favoured Races in the Struggle for Life. Origin is the most elegant theory advanc-ing evolution.

RAYMOND

Darwin admitted that, any complex organ-ism existed that could not have been formed by slight, successive modifica-tions, his theory would break down.

FRED

Then you have read *The Origin?*

RAYMOND

Yes. Darwin was a great thinker, but

unfortunately, I found *The Origin* as dull
as a doorstop.

(Fred stands and begins strutting.)

FRED

The Origin of Species propelled an intel-
lectual revolution. Descent with modifi-
cation through natural selection happens
in small steps within a population, which
are barely noticeable from century to
century. *Origin* is one of the most influ-
ential books that science has ever seen
advancing the theory of evolution. As a
result, Darwinism shook the Christian
world and continues to rock its foundations. Darwin's theory is the pillar of
evolutionary biology. But, more importantly, Darwinism is the inspiration for
many who seek evolutionary answers of
non-life to life.
        (He stands over Raymond.)
As I have always said, it is not what
Darwin did not understand, but rather
what he inspired.
        (He returns to the sofa.)
Hydrothermal vents deep on the ocean
floor, spewing out minerals, are excellent candidates for fueling the formation
of organic molecules, the building blocks
that produced primitive life on earth.
Why, even the ancient Greek philosophers
postulated that life came from non-life,

and man descended from animals.

    (Elizabeth and Christine enter.
    Elizabeth sits next to Fred. Chris-
    tine sits in the armchair across
    from Raymond.)

RAYMOND

To trust evolution ignores what we've
gained through twenty-first-century technology. As a result, the Darwinian paradigm is technologically obsolete.

FRED

We have come a long way since Darwin.
However, if Darwinism is obsolete, why
are we still arguing over his theory?

RAYMOND

Because the alternative would be to
acknowledge God exists.

CHRISTINE

It doesn't take religion or a biologist
to see Darwinism as an antiquated theory
based on nineteenth-century science.

FRED

Again, my argument is that it is not
about what Darwin did not understand, but
rather about what he inspired.

CHRISTINE

I think it is notable that just through observation, Darwin understood how organisms adapt to their environment by microsteps, the variation of finches' beaks—

RAYMOND

Yes, variations within the same species. A wolf into a dog, or a tiger into a cuddly, domesticated housecat.

FRED

Carl Sagan said, "The environment selects those mutations that enhance survival, resulting in a series of slow transformations of one life form into another. The origin of a new species."

RAYMOND
(He laughs.)
One kind of animal transforming into a different animal, as a mouse evolving into a duck, is as reliable as running on ice.

CHRISTINE

Science, by now, should have uncovered evidence of evolution. Instead, we find gaps in most fossil groups.

FRED
(He stands.)
Nonsense . . . Archaeopteryx is a

transitional fossil linking dinosaurs and
birds.
                    (He sits, fidgeting.)
Pakicetus is a small land mammal linking it to whales by its inner ear shape,
called an auditory bulla.
                    (He pauses.)
Ah, yes . . . Tiktaalik, an ancient fish.
The bones of the fins are homologous to
the human hand and wrist bones.

                    RAYMOND
Darwin's tree of life has no roots.

                    FRED
                (He leaps up.)
Hogwash! I just gave you three.

                    RAYMOND
The Cambrian Explosion was the sudden,
abrupt appearance of fully formed, complex organisms discovered in the fossil
record. However, no legitimate evidence
of ancestral transitional fossils in pre-
ceding layers have ever been found.

                    FRED
Absence does not prove creation! When
peculiarities of the natural world per-
sists in being incomplete, *that* is when
your "God of the gaps" becomes most reliable.

RAYMOND
Yes, I agree. Some Christians operate in
faith by concerning themselves less about
how and why. And there are Christians who
understand God engineered every detail of
creation, inventing the language of mathematics before He spoke.

ELIZABETH
A wise premise: think before you speak.

(Throughout the following, Christine stands, crosses to the serving
table, and pours a coffee.)

FRED
(He sits.)
"The lack of understanding of something
is not evidence for God. It is evidence
of a lack of understanding."

ELIZABETH
Lawrence Krauss . . .

CHRISTINE
Darwin had no idea that a cell is an
assembly of molecular protein machines,
miniature engines. Instead, he and his
peers believed the cell was a simple
homogeneous globule of protoplasm.

ELIZABETH
A little shapeless lump of mucus . . .

                    CHRISTINE
Tiny bags of jelly.

                    RAYMOND
Boogers.

                    ELIZABETH
Raymond, behave.

  (Raymond stands, crossing to Christine.)

                    RAYMOND
Why can't Darwin's chickens cross the
road?

                    CHRISTINE
I don't know. Why can't Darwin's chickens
cross the road?

                    RAYMOND
Because evolution takes millions to billions of years, his chickens randomly
mutate into roadkill.

  *(Dude barks. Christine and Raymond
  return to their seats.)*

                    RAYMOND
A single cell is similar to a city, with
highways, byways, and infrastructure
operating twenty-four hours a day, seven
days a week, three-hundred sixty-five days
a year. You speak of Christians living

in the dark ages; haven't you seen the
videos on the cell?

                    FRED
              (He stands.)
Yes, and again, the argument is not about
what Darwin did not understand, but
instead about what he inspired.
              (He begins pacing.)
Simply put, we now possess the knowledge of how non-coding DNA, what we pre-
supposed as genetically flawed junk,
functions as switches, turning existing protein genes on and off at different
intervals and durations, with diverse
intensities that can cause genetic alterations. Through natural selection, these
genetic alterations are then passed onto
individuals that become advantageous for
the survival of a population.
              (He sits on the sofa.)
And they establish a pattern of how one
species, over much time, slowly transi-
tions into a new species.

                    RAYMOND
Yes, a fruit fly and an elephant with the
same grandparents are one big leap of the
imagination and one giant step for muta-
tion.

                    FRED
Raymond, may I remind you that you had

difficulty with the natural sciences and
biology in college?

ELIZABETH
And may I remind you both that *neither* of
you is a biologist.

RAYMOND
Yes, but today, brilliant creation scientists are leading the way in educat-
ing the general public that new scientific
discoveries are pointing to the Biblical
account.

CHRISTINE
I respect how unpretentiously Michael
Behe describes his work. I'll paraphrase.
Irreducible complexity is how a single
system is composed of several interacting
parts and where the removal of any one of
the parts causes the system to stop functioning.

RAYMOND
That sounds like it settles the chicken-
or-the-egg dilemma.

(Raymond begins scrolling on his
phone.)

ELIZABETH
As I understand, instead of irreducible
complexity, Behe now prefers the phrase,
"purposeful arrangement of parts."

CHRISTINE
Behe demonstrates his theory through the
example of a mousetrap. By removing any
part of this simple mechanism, the whole
system will cease functioning for what it
was designed to accomplish.

FRED
In peer-reviewed journals, the scientific
community rejects Behe's theory as pseu-
doscientific.

RAYMOND
Yes, a conspiracy of peer pressure.
Either publicly reject Behe's work, or we
will eliminate your funding, and you can
forget about tenure.

FRED
Irreducible complexity and intelligent
design are fundamental in defending creationism. Therefore, associating the Biblical account in any form as science is
fallacious.

RAYMOND
Stephen Meyer wrote:
        (*He reads from his phone.*)

"At the close of the nineteenth century, most biologists thought life con-
sisted solely of matter and energy. But
after Watson and Crick, biologists came
to recognize the importance of a third
fundamental entity in living things:
information."

CHRISTINE
(She leaps up.)
Yes. Intelligent design is based on the
concept that DNA functions as a language,
similar to arranging letters, images, or
symbols to communicate information in
precise ways.
(Allegro.)
Comparable to computer codes, Morse
codes, barcodes, tax codes, building codes, fire codes, zip codes, texts
sent on your phone, or notes on small
pieces of scrap paper Lizzy leaves on the
refrigerator to remind you to pick up the
dry cleaning on your way home. No form
of communication, be it sign language,
spoken, or written, can randomly change
its characters within the sequence and
continue to communicate meaningful information.
(Enthusiastically.)
Many essential thoughts working to form
one great idea!

RAYMOND
Wow, Chris. If you're this passion-
ate about intelligent design, you must
believe in a creator.

CHRISTINE
(She sits.)
Intelligent design is not a theory of
creation. Instead, it is based on the
fact that DNA stores information and acts
as a language. It does not need to identify an author.

RAYMOND
"Intelligent design opens the whole pos-
sibility of us being created in the image
of a benevolent God."

ELIZABETH
William Dembski.

FRED
(He stands.)
Raymond, I do not support any pseudosci-
entific flavor you decide to favor . . .
It is understood that man is made from
dirt--

RAYMOND
Dust--

                    FRED
Whatever! My point is: we are composed of
sixty percent water. Do you understand
what happens when you add water to dirt?
                (He sits on the sofa.)
You get mud, comprised of minerals with
the potential to form organic molecules,
the building blocks that produced primitive life on earth.

                    RAYMOND
Freddy, intelligent design is the new
science.

                    ELIZABETH
"Nothing is more powerful than an idea
whose time has come."

                    CHRISTINE
Victor Hugo.
                (She stands.)
I once read, I can't remember where, but
I'll paraphrase: Life on earth is car-
bon-based. Carbon has an atomic number
of six. Six protons, six neutrons, six
electrons, and the number of a man is six
hundred sixty-six.

        *(Everyone stares at Christine for a
        long moment.)*

                    CHRISTINE
I don't have a point . . . Sorry . . .

(She sits.)
I just thought it was an interesting side note.

(The lights go out. Dude barks.)

ELIZABETH *(V.O.)*
"And the Lord God formed man of the dust of the ground and breathed into His nostrils the breath of life, and man became a living soul."

(The lights rise on the vacant room.)

CHRISTINE *(O.S.)*
Lizzy, is something wrong?

ELIZABETH *(O.S.)*
This evening has turned in a way I hoped it wouldn't.

CHRISTINE *(O.S.)*
Are you making me responsible?

(Elizabeth and Christine enter.)

ELIZABETH
No, but I had hoped you would help redirect the conversation. Instead, you joined in and fueled the fire.

                    CHRISTINE
You've contributed to the conversation as
well. Would you rather we chat about the
weather and the good old days?

                    ELIZABETH
We could play a word game, or charades.
Yes, you know Fred likes to play charades.

                    CHRISTINE
               (She sits on the sofa.)
Lizzy, I didn't start the conversation.

        (Elizabeth sits next to Christine.)

                    ELIZABETH
You know, when Fred's uncle and aunt died,
Raymond came to live with Fred's family,
but I'm not sure if you're aware that Raymond went through some difficult times.

                    CHRISTINE
                  (annoyed)
Of course, I'm aware!

                    ELIZABETH
Well, fortunately, the boys were there
for each other and became best friends--

                    CHRISTINE
                (Pointedly.)
Yes, and I vividly remember they referred
to each other as cuz, and how it caught

on with everyone in the neighborhood.
Catch you later, cuz. I got your back,
cuz.
             (Reflecting.)
Huh, that's curious . . . back then, I
thought calling someone "cuz" was an
Italian expression.

                    ELIZABETH
How do you remember?

                    CHRISTINE
What do you mean, "how do I remember?" I
wasn't that young.

                    ELIZABETH
Because you were never around until
later.

                    CHRISTINE
I was too! For Christmas, and a few weeks
over summer vacation.

                    ELIZABETH
Yes, we referred to you as the holiday
cousin.

                    CHRISTINE
             (She stands.)
"Holiday cousin?" That's shameful! Who
called me the holiday cousin? Did Auntie
know you called me the holiday cousin?

ELIZABETH
Mommy started it.

CHRISTINE
(A moment as the revelation sinks in.)
It wasn't my fault! I was a child. I
lived in Brooklyn! At least I came to
visit. Not once did you ever come to see
me!

ELIZABETH
We always look forward to your family's
visits.
(She stands.)
But we digress. My point is that after
the incident, Fred and Raymond hardly
spoke. You know I invited Raymond here,
hoping they would reconnect, but instead,
they're arguing.

CHRISTINE
Lizzy, they're adults and can make their
own decisions. Holiday cousin? Give me a
break.

(The lights fade out to black.)

CHRISTINE *(V.O.)*
"For you formed my inward parts; you
knitted me together in my mother's womb.
I praise you, for I am fearfully and won-
derfully made. Wonderful are your works;
my soul knows it very well."

(The lights slowly rise on Elizabeth, silently reading from her iPad, while Fred flips pages of an oversized book. Both are seated in armchairs. A long pause.)

FRED

Ah . . . Here 'tiz . . .
          (He reads aloud.)
"Biologists must constantly keep in mind that what they see was not designed, but rather evolved."

(Fred looks at his wife, but she's absorbed with her iPad.)

FRED

(He reads aloud, an octave louder.)
"Biologists must constantly keep in mind that what they see was not designed, but rather evolved!"

ELIZABETH

(Still staring at her iPad.)
Are you speaking to me?

FRED

Yes. Can you name that quote?

(She ignores him.)

                         FRED
                      (Annoyed.)
Would you like me to repeat the quote?

            (Silence. Fred stands, crossing to
            his wife. A long moment, but she
            continues to ignore him.)

                         FRED
                   (He blurts out.)
Raymond started it!

                       ELIZABETH
               (She looks up, sharply.)
What?

                         FRED
                  (He crosses back.)
You heard me!

            (Fred sits. Elizabeth gazes at her
            husband for a moment.)

                       ELIZABETH
Fred, grow up! You need to be the mature
brother, agree to disagree, and learn to
move on.

            (She returns to her iPad. A pause.)

                       ELIZABETH
                    (She looks up.)
I don't want things to end unpleasantly,

like last time. Make peace with him.
Please . . .

(Fred taps with his finger on the
arms of the chair. Then, working on
sounding casual:)

FRED
Ah . . . What are you reading?

ELIZABETH
An article . . . "Twenty-six reasons why
husbands act stupidly." Would you like me
to send you the link, dear?

(Fred stands, begins pacing. Elizabeth deliberately ignores him
again. Then, after a long moment,
she looks up.)

ELIZABETH
Fred, I understand you're hurt—

FRED
He acts like he knows better . . .

ELIZABETH
. . . and angry—

FRED
Little brother, giving me advice . . .

                    ELIZABETH
. . . because Raymond doesn't need you to
protect him anymore--

                      FRED
Look at me; I memorized all the verses...

                    ELIZABETH
. . . and that's a good thing.

        (Fred plops down into the chair.)

                      FRED
Self-righteous, hypocritical . . .
Dreamer! I think Raymond enjoys his igno-
rance.

           (A long pause passes.)

                    ELIZABETH
You know I'm right!

        *(Fred looks up at the ceiling, then
        at his wife. He stands, then plops
        back down. A long moment passes as
        Elizabeth glares and he sulks.)*

                    ELIZABETH
Take Dude for a walk.

        *(We hear the front door opening,
        then closing, over Christine and
        Raymond.)*

                    CHRISTINE *(O.S.)*
. . . remember Tommy Fuller?

                    RAYMOND *(O.S.)*
Was he that tall skinny kid?

                    CHRISTINE *(O.S.)*
No, that was his brother, Phillip. Tommy
had a severe acne problem.

                    RAYMOND *(O.S.)*
I used to feel bad for him . . .

                    (They enter.)

                    RAYMOND
                    (Upbeat.)
Hello, everyone . . .

                    ELIZABETH
Did you have a pleasant walk?

                    CHRISTINE
                    (She sits.)
Ray bought me ice cream.

                    RAYMOND
Going through the neighborhood brought me
back to the old days.

                    ELIZABETH
Well, I'm glad you kids had fun . . .

(Raymond crosses to Fred.)

RAYMOND
(Upbeat.)
What are you reading?

FRED
A quote that clearly defines the standard
operating procedure.
(He reads aloud.)
"Biologists must constantly keep in mind
that what they see was not designed, but
rather evolved."

RAYMOND
Francis Crick . . . Yes, that's similar
to saying a school bus driver must constantly keep in mind that when a stop-
light turns red, they must consciously
make an effort to remember to read the
instructions for when and how to apply
the brakes.

*(Raymond laughs. Fred stands and
angrily slams the book on the floor,
startling everyone and causing Dude
to Bark.)*

ELIZABETH
Fred! Really?

*(Elizabeth stands and exits. Ray-
mond follows her out. A moment*

passes, then Fred sits.)

FRED
Christine, may I continue?

CHRISTINE
Well, I--

FRED
(Over-the-top, loud.)
The appearance of design in nature is
atoms arranging themselves in a prede-
termined state. So it is that molecules
necessitate equilibrium by forming geometric structures. The delicate symmetry of
snowflakes -- not one the same -- reflects
electrically charged particles' molecular
order. So it is the atomic order, which
gives the impression of being designed but
instead has evolved . . .

*(Elizabeth and Raymond reenter with
cake and plates, crossing to the
serving table.)*

FRED
. . . The proof of the pudding is when a
double helix DNA molecule is suspended in
a liquid that evaporates. What is left
behind are geometric patterns, similar
to inorganic crystals. So, yes, it is a
viable hypothesis that life could have
emerged somehow assisted by crystals.

                    RAYMOND
You can't get blood out of a stone; of
course, evolutionists will disagree with
the premise.

                    ELIZABETH
Fruitcake, anyone?

          (The lights go out. Dude Barks.)

                  RAYMOND (V.O.)
"Train up a child in the way he should
go, and when he is old, he will not
depart from it."

          (The lights rise on everyone stand-
          ing at the serving table. Fred is
          eating cake.)

                    RAYMOND
Chris, do you teach evolution in your
class?

                    CHRISTINE
Yes, teachers are required to follow
everything outlined in the textbooks. The
school board does not allow any deviation
from the regulations.

FRED

I suppose you support teaching creationism in public schools?

CHRISTINE

I didn't say that! I'm saying that we
shouldn't be mandated to teach a theory
that has been progressively proven out-
dated without bringing the existing scientific ideas to the table.

RAYMOND

If they allow evolution to be taught in
public schools, why not recognize intelligent design?

FRED

The United States Supreme Court has ruled
that teaching creationism as science in
public schools is unconstitutional.

RAYMOND

And believing in evolution isn't a religion?

CHRISTINE
(She sits on the sofa.)
Once, I asked our principal if I could
share Stephen Meyer's YouTube video,
"Signature in the Cell." And . . . I
imagined it would be insightful in many
ways to demonstrate Michael Behe's theory
of irreducible complexity.

> FRED
> *(Pointedly.)*

How? By handing out mousetraps to third
graders as a hands-on activity?

> *(Fred, with a plate of fruitcake,
> exits.)*

> ELIZABETH
> *(She calls after him.)*

Fred, you shouldn't feed fruitcake to a
dog.

> RAYMOND

What did the principal say about the video?

> *(Dude barks.)*

> CHRISTINE

That showing the video to my class could
jeopardize my teaching position. I wanted
to see how far I could push the envelope
to understand my boundaries. It kills me
to have to mislead my kids.
> *(She stands.)*

It's a shame; our children are taught
evolution from preschool and are told
that anything else is considered radi-
cally wrong.

> RAYMOND

I was inspired by a quote I read by Sean
McDowell: "It is a humbling thought that

our character and our relationships with
young people can shape their understanding of God."
(He pauses.)
In my sculpture classes, students like
talking about the meaning behind their
work. So I speak about my work and how
it relates to my Christian faith . . . I
witness, by default.

ELIZABETH
Open with care; intelligence is required.

CHRISTINE
Children, please take these release forms
home; I don't want to become unemployed
and have to move back to my mom's house
in Brooklyn.

ELIZABETH
"A new scientific truth does not triumph
by convincing its opponents and making
them see the light, but rather because
its opponents eventually die . . ."

CHRISTINE
Max Planck . . .

RAYMOND
Intelligent design is the new science.

(A pause.)

ELIZABETH

Raymond, thank you for endeavoring to open
your brother's heart to the truth. Heaven
knows how hard I've tried to get Fred to
come to church. But it would have been
considerate if you enabled him to witness
how you've grown rather than pressuring
him into a new way of thinking. So now,
please excuse me. I need to assist my husband in putting things into perspective.

(Elizabeth exits. Dude barks.)

RAYMOND

That's one of the things I love about
Liz; you always know where you stand.

CHRISTINE
(She sits.)
I spend my days with third graders, and
although they surprise me often, it isn't
intellectually rewarding, most of the
time. I'm enjoying our conversation.

(He sits next to her on the sofa.)

RAYMOND

Chris. If you acknowledge intelligent
design, then you must believe in God. Or
aliens.

CHRISTINE

Well, I don't believe in aliens, and as

far as God is concerned, that option is
still on the table.
>> *(She pauses.)*
So why did you become a Christian?

>> RAYMOND

The long or short version?

>> CHRISTINE

Short, please.

>> RAYMOND

I don't know if you remember, but growing
up, I was always in trouble--

>> CHRISTINE
>> *(Annoyed.)*

Of course, I remember!
>> *(She pauses.)*
Sorry . . . Yes, you were a wise guy, but
we had a lot of fun, and . . . is this
the short version?

>> RAYMOND

It's funny how fast the fun runs out when
you owe money to people you never want to
owe anything.
>> *(He stands.)*
I was in a panic. I had hardly slept or
eaten in a day or two. I was wandering
downtown, literally planning to change my
name and zip code.
>> *(He paces.)*

This young kid was handing out flyers,
telling people about Jesus. As I passed
by, he handed me one; I shoved it in my
pocket and forgot about it. That night,
while emptying my pockets, well, printed
on the flyer, was a question: When you die
and meet God, will you wish you had prepared more for eternity?

(He sits.)

Later, I found out it was expressed by
John Lennox. Anyway, the question was
like a slap in the face. I've spent my
life spinning wheels, lying to myself,
being a victim, blaming others, and
accusing God without ever knowing him.

(He pauses.)

I broke down, kneeling on the floor and
praying. I don't know for how long, but I
was exhausted and fell asleep.

(He pauses.)

When I woke, it was morning. I was fam-
ished, put a pot of coffee on, and real-
ized I wasn't anxious. Something changed.
I didn't feel alone; it wasn't about me
anymore.

*(Christine vigorously rubs both her
arms.)*

CHRISTINE
Wow! I just got goosebumps!

(A pause.)

RAYMOND

That young man's name is Brian. He and
many other amazing people became my new
friends and helped me accept God into my
life.

CHRISTINE

What happened with the money you owed?

RAYMOND

I paid it back. It was a challenging but
invaluable lesson.
(He pauses.)
Chris, it doesn't make sense to acknowledge intelligent design as science and
dismiss God as the author.

CHRISTINE

Before I began teaching, I accepted the
idea of how we're made of star-stuff
because the experts knew better than me.
But because I'm required to teach evolution, and since I began reading about
intelligent design, the more I understand
the evolutionary paradigm is a fallacy, a
lie.

RAYMOND

Yes, but you must believe in something
beyond materialism?

CHRISTINE

Why is it important to you that I accept
God in my life?

RAYMOND

Either you allow God's word to guide you,
or you enable the world to control you.

(Christine stands, her back to him.)

CHRISTINE

Well, maybe, perhaps, the Christian life-
style comes with a little too much baggage.

RAYMOND
(He stands.)
Instead of baggage, think of our Savior
arriving with gifts.

CHRISTINE

I guess I'm reluctant to let go of certain things, and that would make me a
hypocrite.
(She pauses.)
It's a commitment I'm unwilling to make
at this time.
(She faces him.)
But hearing you speak with such convic-
tion . . . I can't avoid feeling con-
victed . . . Ray, how do you . . . toe
the line?

                    RAYMOND
I don't always, particularly when driving
behind a slowpoke who keeps braking going
uphill.
                  (He pauses.)
What is necessary for me is reading the
Word daily and hanging out with other
believers.

                    CHRISTINE
Ray, you've given me much to consider . . .

                    RAYMOND
Chris, when you're ready -- and I know
you will be -- I'll walk you through
receiving the gift of salvation.

            (The lights go out.)

              ELIZABETH (V.O.)
"All scripture is given by inspiration of
God and is profitable for doctrine, for
reproof, for correction, for instruction
in righteousness that the man of God may
be perfect, thoroughly furnished to all
good works."

    (The lights rise on everyone,
    seated. A moment. Fred stands, then
    crosses to Raymond.)

                    FRED
Raymond, our positions have reached a

standoff. I am willing to agree to disagree and move on.

                    RAYMOND
                (He stands.)
As I told you before, I will not compromise on God's word.

            (Fred is taken aback.)

                    FRED
                (Pointedly.)
Yes, I am confident of your good intentions when you latch onto notions. Not
unlike when you dashed off to Vegas . . .

                  ELIZABETH
          (She shouts, leaping up.)
Fred--!

                    FRED
. . . with a surefire strategy of winning
at blackjack, and I had to bail you out.

                  ELIZABETH
Fred! Please . . .

                    FRED
. . . It is just another phase; next
week, it will be something else. I have
had enough of this hypocrisy of spewing
out learned-by-heart Bible verses--

ELIZABETH

Fred-stop-talking!

*(Fred crosses to exit, stops,
turns, crosses back to Raymond.)*

FRED

Although, little brother, may I offer one
last piece of advice? As a teacher, your
students adhere to your words as instruction. But sadly, it only takes one indi-
vidual to make an accusation. So be
mindful of professing your faith.

*(Fred exits. The lights go out.
Dude barks.)*

END ACT I

ACT II

*(The lights slowly rise on the
vacant living room.)*

RAYMOND *(V.O.)*
"In the beginning, God created the heaven
and the earth. And the earth was without
form and void, and darkness was upon the
face of the deep. And the Spirit of God
moved upon the face of the waters. And
God said, Let there be light: and there
was light. And God saw the light, that it
was good: and God divided the light from
the darkness. And God called the light
Day, and the darkness he called Night.
And the evening and the morning were the
first day."

(A moment passes.)

ELIZABETH *(O.S.)*
Yes, I know.
(She pauses.)
Very stubborn.
(She pauses.)
No, he still refuses to talk about it.

*(Elizabeth enters, holding a cell
phone to her ear.)*

ELIZABETH
Yes, be a dear. Five thirty.

(*She pauses.*)
Fred usually pulls in around six and, try
not to be late. Bye-bye.

> (*Lights out. A moment passes, then
> the doorbell chimes, and Dude
> barks. Lights rise on the vacant
> room.*)

ELIZABETH (*O.S.*)
Dude, behave; it's only Christine. Lie
down.

> (*We hear the front door opening.*)

ELIZABETH (*O.S.*)
You're late.

CHRISTINE (*O.S.*)
Traffic is terrible.

ELIZABETH (*O.S.*)
Let me take your coat.

CHRISTINE (*O.S.*)
Hello Dude, are you being a good boy?

> (*We hear the front door closing.*)

CHRISTINE (*O.S.*)
Is Fred home?

                    ELIZABETH *(O.S.)*
Do you see his car?

                    CHRISTINE *(O.S.)*
Then I'm not late . . .

        (They enter, crossing to the serving
        table. Elizabeth fills a coffee cup.)

                    CHRISTINE
So, what's the game plan?

                    ELIZABETH
        (She hands Christine the cup.)
"The game plan." Are we in grade school?

                    CHRISTINE
Lizzy, you at least should have told Fred
you invited me to dinner.

                    ELIZABETH
Perhaps, but I'm sure my husband was
counting on me inviting Raymond back.

        (They sit together on the sofa.)

                    CHRISTINE
Well, you know better.

                (Dude barks.)

                    ELIZABETH
Fred's home . . .

(We hear the front door open-
ing, then closing, and Dude barks
again.)

                    FRED *(O.S.)*
                  (Sing-song.)
Big boy, what are you going to do, what
are you to do when they come for you?
                  (Loudly.)
Elizabeth, whose car is in the driveway?
     (Improvisation of master and dog
     playing)
Who is the Dude? Who is the Dude? Yes, my
boy. We are going for a walk, give me a
minute.

          (Fred enters.)

               CHRISTINE
Hello, Fred.

                  FRED
Christine, is that your Lexus?

               CHRISTINE
I just bought it. Do you like it?

                  FRED
Pricey, for an elementary school salary.

               CHRISTINE
I work hard, and I deserve it.

(Fred sits in one of the armchairs.)

FRED

So, Christine, what special occasion has motivated you to brave cross-city traffic?

CHRISTINE

Does there have to be a special occasion for a visit?

ELIZABETH

Fred. I've something to tell you.

FRED

It must be significant, if you need to announce your intentions along with a witness . . . Wait, Christine, the last time you visited . . .
(To Elizabeth.)
Is Raymond on his way?

ELIZABETH

Yes, I invited him.

FRED

So he may bestow his blessings on us?

(Christine laughs.)

FRED

Do you find this funny?

CHRISTINE
I found Raymond's last visit very inspir-
ing.
(She holds out her cup.)
Fred, please be a dear. Refresh my coffee?

(Throughout the following, Fred
stands, takes the cup, crosses to
the serving table, refills the cup,
then returns to Christine.)

ELIZABETH
A day is a day, and the years pass
quickly. Then one day, we look back on
those years as the good old days. Yes,
a reason they are good is that "Today
is the oldest you've ever been, and the
youngest you'll ever be again."

CHRISTINE
(She takes the cup.)
Eleanor Roosevelt . . .

ELIZABETH
Fred, today, make peace with him.

(The lights slowly fade out to black.)

ELIZABETH (V.O.)
". . . In these last days, He has spoken
to us by His Son, whom He appointed heir
of all things, and through whom also He
made the universe."

*(The lights rise. Elizabeth and
Fred are seated in armchairs.
Christine and Raymond are sitting
on the sofa. Raymond is nervously
tapping his fingers.)*

ELIZABETH

Are you sure I can't get you anything?

RAYMOND

Yes, I'm sure.

ELIZABETH

Perhaps some seltzer, maybe a little
fruit juice--?

FRED

Elizabeth, he does not want anything!

CHRISTINE

Ray, did you accept the Chair position--?

(Raymond shifts with discomfort.)

ELIZABETH

Oh, the Department of Mathematics nomi-
nated Fred for tenure.

RAYMOND

Well, good for you.

CHRISTINE

Yes, congratulations.

                    FRED
It is not official yet, but I am a shoo-in,
and thank you both.

                  RAYMOND
You must be doing an exceptional job. The
powers that be don't grant tenure privi-
leges to just anyone. Of course, one must
never question the official academic
dogma . . .

                    FRED
What you call "official academic dogma" is
based on science.

                 CHRISTINE
You boys just jump right in--

                    FRED
Raymond, I do not intend to go round in
circles with you.

                  RAYMOND
We both know we have rehearsed what we
wished we had said, or didn't . . .
                 (He stands.)
Freddy. It's time we finish our conversation.

     *(Fred looks from Raymond to his
     wife, then back to Raymond and
     stands.)*

FRED
Raymond. If you insist.

(*The lights go out. Dude barks.*)

CHRISTINE *(V.O.)*
"Where were you when I laid the foundations
of the earth? Tell Me if you have understanding. Who determined its measurements?
Surely you know! Or who stretched the line
upon it? To what were its foundations fas-
tened? Or who laid its cornerstone when the
morning stars sang together, and all the
sons of God shouted for joy?"

(*The lights rise on Fred and Raymond, seated in armchairs. Raymond
is scrolling on his phone.*)

FRED
Is Genesis History? Does the language of
Genesis draw a reliable blueprint detail-
ing how the universe was built? Earth was
made before the stars?
(*He pauses.*)
Genesis is analytically problematic.

RAYMOND
Isaac Newton said, "This most beautiful
system of the sun, planets, and comets
could only proceed from the counsel and
dominion of an intelligent and powerful
Being."

FRED

Raymond. Our galaxy is just one of the
billions scattered throughout the infinite
expanse. The earth is an insignificant
speck lost in the delusion of significance.

RAYMOND

A quote by Robert Jastrow.
    (He reads from his phone.)
"At this moment, it seems as though science will never be able to raise the curtain on the mystery of creation. For the
scientist who has lived by his faith in
the power of reason, the story ends like
a bad dream. He has scaled the mountains
of ignorance; he is about to conquer the
highest peak; as he pulls himself over
the final rock, he is greeted by a band of
theologians who have been sitting there
for centuries."

FRED

Carl Sagan said, "The cosmos is within
us. We are made of star-stuff. We are a
way for the universe to know itself."
Cosmic evolution is undeniable.

RAYMOND

"The heavens declare the glory of God,
and the firmament shows His handiwork--"

    *(Elizabeth and Christine enter and
    sit on the sofa.)*

                    FRED
Indeed, the firmament. Please explain what
a firmament is?

    (Fred removes a small pad from
    his inside jacket pocket and flips
    pages.)

                    RAYMOND
"And God said, Let there be a firmament
in the depth of the waters, and let it
divide the waters from the waters. And
God made the firmament, and divided the
waters which were under the firmament from
the waters which were above the firmament: and it was so. And God called the
firmament Heaven. And the evening and the
morning were the second day."

                    FRED
May you explain the secrets of Genesis?
Clearly, via memorizing the verse.

                    RAYMOND
The firmament looks to be space itself
that divides the waters into two parts.
One part remains the earth's waters, and
the other consists of the waters being
stretched out to the edge of the observable universe, effectively forming the
expanse, the cosmos.

FRED

May you solve the mysteries of creation?
Most certainly, by circular reasoning,
you may.

RAYMOND

The Word states seventeen times that the
Lord stretches out the heavens. What if
the waters expanding outward is the embod-
iment of microwave background radiation?

FRED

Well, Raymond, that certainly is an
interesting thought experiment, but thin.

RAYMOND

"The Lord wraps himself in light as with
a garment; He stretches out the heavens like a tent and lays the beams of His
upper chambers on the waters . . ."
                (He pauses)
In the beginning, what if the earth was a
gigantic, formless mass of water? Then,
like Michelangelo chiseling away the
extra material from the marble block,
sculpting the image he sees in his mind's
eye, God shaped and formed this mass into
a watery sphere. And the excess water,
cast it away from His masterpiece creat-
ing the firmament, the cosmos, the second
heaven. And the waters above became the
dome of blackbody radiation of the cosmic
microwave background we see today.

                    FRED
A very ambitious sculpture project. To
say the least.

                  (A pause.)

                    FRED
Revelation states that stars will fall to
the earth. So how could stars fall and
land on our planet, without the world
being vaporized? End of story!

                  RAYMOND
Meteors--

                    FRED
Meteors . . . ? I see . . .
          (He reads from his pad.)
". . . and the stars in the sky fell to
earth, as figs drop from a fig tree when
shaken by a strong wind."

                  RAYMOND
Freddy, I'm delighted you studied for our
debate.

                  ELIZABETH
"A voice said, look me in the stars and
tell me truly men of earth if all the
soul-and-body scars were not too much to
pay for birth."

                    CHRISTINE
Robert Frost . . . Lizzy, remember when
we were children, we would try and count
the stars.

                    ELIZABETH
Yes, we would start counting over
here . . .

                    CHRISTINE
Get lost over there . . .

                    ELIZABETH
Then we would have to start counting all
over again.

                    RAYMOND
"And God said, Let there be lights in
the firmament of the heaven to divide the
day from the night, and let them be for
signs, and seasons, and for days, and
years. And let them be for lights in the
firmament of the heaven to give light on
the earth, and it was so."

                     FRED
Yes, all well and good, but the book of
Genesis does not clearly define what a
star is, nevertheless galaxies.

                    RAYMOND
                 (He stands.)
What if God constructed the cosmos as the

mechanism for keeping time. Wheels and gears, fine-tuning and calculating every point. A supernova over here, a comet over there, and galaxies everywhere. I imagine it takes a big gravitational engine to move physical space-time forward, and God invented it for His purpose.

                    FRED
And perhaps the arrow of time is just an illusion. But, yes, I have always found your thought experiments extremely entertaining. The universe as one big clock, tick-tock.

                  RAYMOND
"And God made two great lights, the greater light to rule the day, and the lesser light to rule the night, and He made the stars also."

                    FRED
                (Pointedly.)
Did "He make the stars also?"

     (Fred leaps up, tearing a page from his pad. He holds it out, shaking it at Raymond.)

                    FRED
Billions of galaxies and trillions of
stars . . . What is this "also" business?
I will tell you; it is dismissive. Using
the word also, the author had no idea
what those points of light in the sky
are, let alone their function.

                    RAYMOND
"There is one glory of the sun, another
glory of the moon, and another glory
of the stars, for one star differs from
another star in glory." It wasn't until
the invention of the telescope that we
understood stars are diverse, falling
into different classifications and sizes.
Yet, the Bible tells us so.

                    FRED
Genesis is the deal-breaker, and it
begins on page one.

                    RAYMOND
Earth is where the story begins. Salvation
is what the story is about, and Jesus, the
Word of God, is the story's hero.

                    FRED
Words of faith in defiance of science . . .

                    RAYMOND
Ask, seek, and knock in defiance of doubt
. . . "For by Him, all things were

created, in heaven and on earth, visible and invisible . . ."
                    (He sits.)
The cosmos is made up of invisible particles and, along with the physical constant--

                    FRED

Stop! I am well acquainted with the prevailing argument regarding fine-tuning in the laws of physics.
            (He crosses to Raymond.)
However, because the universe is well balanced, it does not point to a creator. Life as we know it is fine-tuned to the physics in which we evolved.

                    RAYMOND
                (He stands.)
"By faith, we understand that the universe was created by the word of God so that what is seen was not made out of things that are visible."

                    FRED

The bottom line is that it is impossible to prove the universe was created, nevertheless the existence of God.

                    RAYMOND

"Without faith, it is impossible to please him, for he who comes to God must believe that he is--"

FRED

I do not entertain such faith.

RAYMOND

God made, formed, and created the earth
not in vain but to be inhabited, engineered for life.

FRED

I cannot see anything remotely scientific
in the language of the Bible.

RAYMOND

"For the invisible things of Him from the
creation of the world are clearly seen,
being understood by the things that are
made, even His eternal power and Godhead;
so that they are without excuse."

FRED

A statement attributed to Galileo: "The
Bible tells us how to go to Heaven, not
how the heavens go."

RAYMOND

"Gravity explains the motion of the planets, but it cannot explain who set the
planets in motion." Isaac Newton.

FRED

The great theoretical physicist and cos-
mologist Stephen Hawking said . . . "The
role played by time at the beginning of

the universe is, I believe, the final key to removing the need for a Grand Designer and revealing how the universe created itself."

                    RAYMOND
Yes, Hawking was a great theoreti-
cal physicist, but that is what Hawking believed, not what he could prove. "In the beginning God created . . ." Time, space, and matter in six days.

                    FRED
Raymond, how can you entertain the idea of a six-day creation?

                    RAYMOND
To say that God needed millions or bil-
lions of years acknowledges a form of evolution and deception.

                    FRED
Thousands of years versus billions of years is problematic.

                    RAYMOND
God warns about adding or taking away from His Word. And adding even one more hour to six days of creation leads to a form of evolution and deception.
                 (He pauses.)
It isn't written, "In the beginning, God." However . . .

                    FRED

If the universe is six thousand years
old, how can we see the light from stars
billions of lightyears away?

                  RAYMOND
                (He sits.)
"And God said, Let there be light, and
there was light."

                    FRED

Yes, I am certain . . . However, the math
for the distance of the light to travel
in a six-thousand-year universe does not
add up, whereas uncertainty is eliminated
through more time in billions of years.

                  RAYMOND

"I form the light and create darkness."
Light is made up of electromagnetic radiation, radio waves, gamma--

                    FRED

Yes, yes, I do not need a lesson in Science 101--

                  RAYMOND

"Where is the way where light dwells
. . . ?" 186,000 miles per second . . .

                    FRED

Yes, the speed of light *confirms* my argument against a six-day creation.

                    RAYMOND
What if God, in eternity past, conceived
the cosmos complete, and when He spoke,
the universe came into existence in a
form that is billions of years old? In
the same way, everything in creation was
made fully mature. Then from that moment,
everything proceeds forward in real time.

                     FRED
Raymond, enough with the what-ifs. . .
You are giving me a migraine.

                    RAYMOND
God is beyond the three spatial dimen-
sions and time. We walk by faith, not by
sight.

                     FRED
I rationally will not accept the notion
of a six-day creation any more than I
would receive advice from a millennial.

    (The lights begin to fade out slowly.)

                    RAYMOND
"Where is the way where light dwells, and
as for darkness, where is its place?"
Light waves travel through the darkness of created space, and the vacuum is
unable to prevent light from carrying
its energy along . . . "And God saw the
light, that it was good: and God divided

the light from the darkness. And God called the light Day, and the darkness He called Night. And the evening and the morning were the first day."

(The lights go out.)

RAYMOND *(V.O.)*
"When I consider Your heavens, the work of Your fingers, the moon, and the stars, which You have ordained, what is a man that You are mindful of him, and the son of man that You visit him? For You have made him a little lower than the angels and have crowned him with glory and honor. You have made him have dominion over the works of Your hands and have put all things under his feet."

(The lights rise on everyone
seated. Fred and Elizabeth are
on the sofa when Fred stands and
begins strutting.)

FRED
In the beginning was the Big Bang, the singularity-point, a period on the page, hot and dense, and immediately experiencing rapid inflation. And 380,000 years later, the universe cooled and became transparent, forming the oldest light in the cosmos, filling all space . . . Then, on Wednesday, May 20, 1964, American radio

astronomers Arno Penzias and Robert Wilson detected these microwave emissions emanating from the sky. They first thought the static from their antenna to be bird poop. But by some sweeping and scrubbing, the Bell Labs Holmdel Horn Antenna determined the noise was coming from outside our galaxy.

(He stands over Raymond.)

This discovery earned Penzias and Wilson the 1978 Nobel Prize in Physics.

                    ELIZABETH

Fred. Would you please stop acting pompous? It isn't pleasant.

(Fred returns to the sofa.)

                    ELIZABETH

I witness the consequences of a big bang after my husband showers or makes dinner, and please never allow him to do laundry.

(She smiles.)

Isn't that reasonable, dear?

                    CHRISTINE

I find it ironic that the father of the Big Bang, Georges Lemátre, was a Belgian Catholic priest.

                    RAYMOND

The only thing real about the Big Bang is that the theory acknowledges that the universe had a beginning.

(He stands, then paces.)

In my opinion, the Big Bang is based on data supported by probabilities, massive, burdensome lifesavers, full of what-ifs that need continuous maintenance, keeping the idea afloat.

(He laughs.)

All in all, that's a lot of dark stuff to sweep under the cosmic rug and still call the universe clean. Genesis and the Big Bang are not the same stories.

ELIZABETH

"But slanting eclipses challenge the sun's glory, and time, which gave the noon sun, now clouds it over."

CHRISTINE

William Shakespeare.

RAYMOND

When did the Big Bang take place? Was it eons before, or immediately after the spirit of God moved over the face of the waters? Or maybe it was on the fourth day? Or maybe there wasn't a Big Bang, only God speaking everything into existence just how it is written, one day at a time . . . Genesis and the Big Bang are not the same stories.

                    FRED

I imagine many things, but do not make
them real. However, we can agree that
Genesis and the Big Bang are not the same
stories. One is based on faith and the
other on science.

                  RAYMOND

The cosmological principle states that
the spatial distribution of matter in the
universe is homogeneous and isotropic,
like cream in coffee. Except, in reality,
it isn't.

                    FRED

Are you referring to the subtle temperature variations of the cosmic microwave
background radiation?

                  RAYMOND

Yes, the Wilkinson Microwave Anisotropy
Probe, NASA's satellite, documented that
the universe doesn't appear uniform. And
the same data was confirmed in March of
2013 by Planck, a European Space Agency
observatory satellite.

                    FRED

Stop! I do not need a cosmological history lesson--

CHRISTINE

Well, I would like the hear more. Please
continue, Ray.

RAYMOND

These satellites detected anisotropic
abnormalities. Small temperature fluctuations within the cosmic microwave background appear to point where creation
began within the neighborhood of our
solar system.

FRED
(Pointedly.)

Yes, subtle warm and cool temperature
fluctuations, one part in a hundred thousand . . . So please do not correlate the
concept of creation to the data furnished
by these satellites.

RAYMOND

It appears our earth occupies a special
place.

FRED

Raymond, that notion is far-fetched and
extremely unlikely.

RAYMOND

The Planck data confirms what the Wilkinson Microwave Anisotropy Probe data
reveals. The large-scale structures

within the universe look to align with
Earth's equator and solar system.

> CHRISTINE
>
> Yes, cosmologists describe these align-
> ments with President George Bush's anal-
> ogy about states that sponsor terrorism.

> RAYMOND
>
> It's associated with terrorism because
> the data contradicts the theory of the
> standard model.

> ELIZABETH
>
> I never liked the president's analogy.

> CHRISTINE
>
> The Axis of Evil?

> ELIZABETH
>
> Yes, the axis. Thank you, Christine. "I
> have always depended on the kindness of
> strangers."

> CHRISTINE
>
> Blanche Dubois.

> (Throughout the following, Ray-
> mond crosses to the bookcase and
> removes the globe. Spinning it, he
> returns.)

                    FRED
The thermal black body radiation of the
CMB is uniform, except for slight . . .
slight abnormalities. Subtle temperature
variations between warm and cool areas.
One part in a hundred thousand.

                 CHRISTINE
The colors in the images of the CMB
remind me of a Jackson Pollock painting.

                 ELIZABETH
                 (Lively.)
"Life is a great big canvas. Throw all
the paint on it you can."

                 CHRISTINE
Pablo Picasso?

                 ELIZABETH
Danny Kaye.

                 CHRISTINE
Who's Danny Kaye?

                    FRED
A comedian from the sixties. And the
colors of the CMB images are overstated.
The color has been enhanced to illustrate
the very subtle temperature variations.
One part in a hundred thousand.

CHRISTINE
(She stands next to Raymond.)
Unfortunately, there isn't ade-
quate information for a layperson
like myself to fully understand these
alignments.

RAYMOND
I admit I don't fully understand the science, but I know what the fuss is over.
. . Large-scale warm and cool structures
align with Earth's equator and solar
system.

ELIZABETH
From what I understand, cosmologists are
completely baffled by these alignments.

FRED
Indeed, there should not be a correlation
of the universe with Earth and the solar
system.

CHRISTINE
So, Ray, tell us what you understand . . .

(Raymond gives the globe to Chris-
tine, and throughout the following
they utilize it, pointing out the
alignments.)

RAYMOND
The cosmic microwave background dipole is

the largest warm and cool structure. It aligns with Earth's equator, the axial tilt, at about 23.44 degrees relative to the orbital plane of the ecliptic.

(Christine demonstrates Earth's equator by spinning the globe.)

                    CHRISTINE
So the largest between-warm-and-cool regions that align with Earth's equator is called the dipole?

                    RAYMOND
Yes. The northern hemisphere of the CMB dipole above the equator is slightly cooler than the southern hemisphere below the equator, which is somewhat warmer.

                    CHRISTINE
So the dipole divides the visible universe in half by warm and cool hemispheres?

                    RAYMOND
Yes, according to the data.
                    (He pauses.)
And the warm and cool structures of the CMB perpendicular to the dipole are called the quadrupole and octupole. And they align with Earth's orbit around the sun, the ecliptic.

                    CHRISTINE
So the quadrupole and octupole perpendicular to the dipole aligns with our solar
system?

                    RAYMOND
According to the data.

                    CHRISTINE
Okay, so warm and cool structures of the
CMB align with the Sun-Earth's ecliptic
plane and Earth's equator?
                (She considers.)
Cosmic structures perpendicular to each
other that form an X?

                    RAYMOND
Yes, alignments that form an axis, and
what the fuss is over.

                    CHRISTINE
It sounds so incredible.
                (She sits.)
"Is this Copernicus coming back to haunt
us?"

                    ELIZABETH
Lawrence Krauss . . .

                    RAYMOND
According to Genesis, and what seems to
be confirmed by the data, creation began
with Earth at ground zero.

FRED

The heliocentric model states that the
earth revolves around the sun. The geocentric theory proposes that the moon,
the sun, and stars orbit around the
earth.
                    (He laughs.)
Certainly, you do not support the geocentric model?

RAYMOND
        (He places the globe on the table.)
Freddy, why would you even consider that
I support the geocentric model?

FRED

Your language argues that Earth is the
center of the universe.

RAYMOND

Earth is where the story begins. Salvation is what the story is about, and
Jesus, the Word of God, is the story's
hero.

FRED
            (He stands.)
There must be a useful explanation we
have yet to identify.

RAYMOND

"The Lord wraps himself in light as with
a garment; He stretches out the heavens

like a tent and lays the beams of His
upper chambers on the waters . . ."

                    FRED
Keeping to the science, just last week, I
read an article with enormous potential
refuting these alignments based on con-
tamination by foreground galactic dust
and energy emissions from our galaxy.
Consequently, these findings are in their
early stages, requiring more highly
sophisticated probes. And to follow
through with any new cosmological project, more scientists will need to come on
board and receive the necessary funding.
So, to consider this topic arguable at
this stage is premature.

                  ELIZABETH
Fred, could there be substantial funding?

                    FRED
Oh, yes, substantial funding, and I imagine Nobel Prizes awarded as well.

                  ELIZABETH
              (She laughs.)
Well, we certainly could afford to redo
the kitchen and guest bathroom.

                    FRED
          (He picks up the globe.)
If anything, these abnormalities have

opened the door for new physics and new math. So it is an exciting time for cosmology and science.
          (*He spins the globe.*)
As hopeful as it may be, the notion that a creator has placed us at a central location designated by the most massive structures of the universe is supported by faith, not science.

                    RAYMOND
          (*He crosses to Fred.*)
Yes, by faith. That's why WMAP and Planck's data haven't ever made front-page news.

                    FRED
Are you implying that cosmologists are sweeping this data under the cosmic rug, as well?

                    RAYMOND
          (*He sits.*)
Yes. They are either ignoring it, hoping it will go away, confused about what to do with it, or grappling with being the first to discredit the data.

                    FRED
Jumping the gun without more information at this stage would be reckless and unprofessional. Sadly, we have nothing to compare these alignments to. Perhaps if .

. . if we sent a probe to a different part
of space, maybe the Andromeda Galaxy, we
would have statistics against measuring
the alignments. So the whole argument is
irrelevant.

    *(Fred sits, placing the globe on
the coffee table.)*

             FRED
Stop and listen to yourself!
        (He grows frustrated.)
Raymond. Grow up, for goodness' sake!

          RAYMOND
"Grow up?"
        (He stands.)
Why can't you ever take me seriously?

            FRED
Raymond, be reasonable. The Bible is not
a science book!

          RAYMOND
      (Pointedly.)
You know as well as I that the experts
work very hard to discredit what could be
a phenomenal discovery supporting creation.

            FRED
      (Pointedly.)
Raymond, you are getting carried away as

you always do. Any legitimate scientists pursuing such research would be jeopardizing their careers!

                    RAYMOND
          (He shouts, pointing a finger.)
The Word speaks boldly to every brilliant, witty, arrogant fool who has said in their heart, "There is No God!"

                     FRED
               (He stands.)
Shouting down, you take me for a fool?
               (He shouts.)
That is why you were terminated; you get an idea in your head, and do not let go--

                  ELIZABETH
          (Leaping up, she shouts.)
Fred!

                    RAYMOND
How do you know I was let go?

                     FRED
I have friends . . .

                  ELIZABETH
Raymond, I'm sorry for my husband's lack of manners--

                     FRED
Do not apologize on my behalf.

ELIZABETH
I apologize for your brother's lack of
graciousness.
(She sits.)
Is that better, dear?

CHRISTINE
Ray, what happened?

(A long moment passes.)

RAYMOND
I was called into the dean's office and
accused of preaching my personal religious beliefs to my class.
(He pauses.)
Ironically, the sequence of events fol-
lowed the narrative outlined in the documentary, Expelled: No Intelligence
Allowed.
(He pauses.)
I am guilty of quoting scripture and,
yes, explaining how it inspires my art-
work. I also quote atheists. One of my
favorites is one by Picasso, "The meaning
of life is to find your gift. The purpose
of life is to give it away." The latter
was not the problem.

FRED
Raymond, I gave you a fair warning. Be
mindful of professing your faith.

(A long moment passes.)

RAYMOND

I'm sorry, I lost my temper. I don't mean
. . . It isn't my intention to act like
I have all the answers. But sometimes,
I feel that I'm one scripture away from
slipping back.
(He pauses.)
There was a time I was like you, wagging
my finger in God's face . . . But I was
wrong. You're wrong.
(He pauses.)
Freddy, I respect you more than anyone I
know . . . I've always looked up to you.
Maybe I've gone about this the wrong way,
but your salvation is essential.

FRED
(He pauses.)
I have always surmised your motives . . .
I apologize; it was insensitive of me to
speak out. But, Raymond, it was a sense-
less misjudgment for you to jeopardize
your career!

RAYMOND

It isn't a good feeling, to be let go.
But it is a privilege to be persecuted
for speaking God's Word.

FRED

So, now what are you going to do?

RAYMOND
"Be anxious for nothing—"

ELIZABETH
". . . And the peace of God, which sur-
passes all understanding, will guard your
hearts and minds through Christ Jesus."

*(Fred crosses to his wife, stands
next to her, and places his hand on
her shoulder.)*

FRED
(To everyone.)
Listening to learned-by-heart Bible
verses, I considered my brother was
acting hypocritically.
(To Raymond.)
However, I have been in error, underes-
timating your commitment. I now see how
Christianity is manifesting your full
potential . . . Raymond, for that, I am
thankful.

(Raymond crosses to Fred.)

RAYMOND
Freddy, over the years, I've caused you
much trouble--

                    FRED
Grief. Because your welfare is always my
concern.

                  RAYMOND
You were always there for me.
                (He pauses.)
I promise from now on to be a better
brother.

                    FRED
Cuz! You were never a bad brother.

 (They hug, pat each other on the back.)

                    FRED
We are getting sidetracked.

          (They separate.)

                    FRED
You see these abnormalities of the CMB
only as an opportunity to promote your
theology. Theists find correlations
because they desire to do so.
                (He pauses.)
Yes, as I prepared for our debate, I will
admit I was taken away by a promise of
more than materialism.
            (He begins pacing.)
How may we occupy a special place within
this infinite universe? How can there be
a conscious awareness of our existence?

Shall we toss aside scientific reasoning
over wishful thinking?
                    (*Reflecting.*)
Notwithstanding, these temperature imbal-
ances may be typical within the limits of
our observation and point to an entirely
different place within the universe when
viewed from that place. Arguably, we shall
never know except by tweaking numbers.

                    RAYMOND
Physicists are in panic, tweaking numbers. Is the theory driving the science,
or is the science driving the theory?

                    ELIZABETH
Bottom-up, top-down, tweak or retweak,
that is the question?

                    CHRISTINE
Yes, the argument is practically Shake-
spearean.

                    FRED
True, we are opposed to the Planck data's
theological implications. Science is
based on observation and experiment, not
faith . . . And realistically, at this
moment, I find my argument compromised due
to the lack of sound, observable data.

                    RAYMOND
But there is a standard of observable
data. At the least, these alignments
deserve an earnest theological consider-
ation.

                     FRED
To say the Sun-Earth is cosmically
aligned with a universe 93 billion lightyears across is comparable to accepting a
single bobbing soda bottle could impact
all the oceans' currents.

        (Raymond crosses to his brother.)

                    RAYMOND
"It is He who sits above the circle of
the earth . . . He stretches out the
north over empty space; He hangs the
earth on nothing."

                     FRED
Perhaps there is more in place than just
poetry, which would make us very significant in the scheme of things.
                (Sotto voce.)
"For God so loved the world . . ."

                    RAYMOND
Yes, in the scheme of things . . . "God
so loved the world."

        *(Raymond pats his brother on the
        shoulder.)*

RAYMOND
Perhaps we find a correlation between creation and the cosmic microwave background
alignments because we desire to do so.
However, "In the beginning, God created
the heaven and the earth" is as trust-
worthy as any explanation.
                    (He pauses.)
"He stretches out the heavens like a tent
and lays the beams of His upper chambers
on the waters."

FRED
Incredible, extraordinary, remarkable.
Congratulations, Raymond. You leave me
unable to speculate beyond adjectives.
                    (He considers.)
Yes, indeed, a plausible Axis of Begin-
ning.

ELIZABETH
Fred, I like that analogy much better.

CHRISTINE
Me too . . .

          (Dude barks. The lights go out.)

ELIZABETH *(V.O.)*
"So the heavens and the earth were fin-
ished, and all the host of them. And on
the seventh day, God ended His work which
He had made; and He rested on the seventh

day from all His work which He had made.
And God blessed the seventh day and sanc-
tified it: because that in it He had
rested from all His work which God created and made."

(The following evening. The Lights
rise on Elizabeth, Christine, and
Raymond standing together.)

CHRISTINE
Ray, on our way to the airport, I would
like you to tell me more about Jesus.

(From his duffle bag, Raymond removes
a Bible and hands it to Christine.)

CHRISTINE
But Ray, it has all your notes . . .

RAYMOND
It's a gift.

CHRISTINE
Thank you . . . I'll cherish it.

RAYMOND
No. Read it.
        (He turns to Elizabeth)
Liz, I thank God every day that you're
here for us.

ELIZABETH

Raymond. You're always in my prayers.

(Elizabeth and Raymond hug as Fred enters.)

FRED

Dude is set for the night.

RAYMOND

Freddy, the Bible is not a science book . . .

FRED

However, science undoubtedly is raising the curtain on the mystery of creation.

RAYMOND

Until our next debate . . .

(The boys hug, pat each other on the back, then Fred turns to Christine.)

FRED

Christine, always a pleasure.

CHRISTINE

Good, because I'll be over Thursday night for Bible study.

(Everyone crosses to exit.)

                    ELIZABETH
Raymond, we're expecting you for Thanks-
giving.

                    CHRISTINE
Holiday brother-in-law.

                    ELIZABETH
Christine, behave.

          (Everyone exits. Dude barks.)

                    FRED *(O.S.)*
Quiet, Big Boy, we are going up shortly.

                    CHRISTINE *(O.S.)*
Lizzy, are we still on for tomorrow?

                    ELIZABETH *(O.S.)*
Yes, and text me when you get home.

          (We hear the front door opening.)

                    CHRISTINE *(O.S.)*
If I don't forget. Bye-bye.

                    ELIZABETH *(O.S.)*
She'll forget.

                    FRED *(O.S.)*
Raymond, call me in the morning.

                    RAYMOND *(O.S.)*
I will. God bless. Bye-bye. . .

                    ELIZABETH *(O.S.)*
Raymond, God bless. Bye-bye . . .

                    RAYMOND *(O.S.)*
Dude, you're a good boy . . .

     *(Dude barks. We hear the front door
     closing. Then Fred and Elizabeth
     reenter.)*

                    FRED
I assume you will expect me to come to
church?

                    ELIZABETH
Life is a kite caught up in the wind--

                    FRED
Yes, I know. We need to let God share
handling the line.

     (Fred begins straightening up.)

                    ELIZABETH
Leave it. We'll clean up in the
morning . . .

FRED

The next thing you know, Raymond will want to get the band back together to play Christian music.

ELIZABETH

That would be lovely, dear.

FRED

I am being sarcastic.

ELIZABETH

And I am humoring you . . .
(She pauses.)
Is it possible these cosmic alignments could confirm creation?

(A moment passes as Fred considers.)

FRED

I am unable to see how. However, at this moment, I will acknowledge . . . Earth is where the story begins. Salvation is what the story is about, and I found faith in the story's hero, the Son of God.

ELIZABETH

Fred, I love you.

FRED

Little bit, I love you too . . .

                    ELIZABETH
Little bit . . . ?
                    (A beat passes.)
You haven't called me by my nickname
since college.

                      FRED
Well, sweetheart, you better get used to
it . . .

     (Elizabeth takes her husband by the
     hand.)

                    ELIZABETH
Come, let's go up . . .

     (As Elizabeth leads her husband to
     exit, Fred turns off the lights.
     Dude barks.)

                    FRED *(V.O.)*
"For God so loved the world that He
gave His only begotten Son, that who-
ever believes in Him should not perish
but have everlasting life." "That if you
confess with your mouth, the Lord Jesus,
and shall believe in your heart that God
raised Him from the dead, you shall be
saved. For with the heart, man believes
to righteousness; and with the mouth,
confession is made to salvation."

                AXIS OF BEGINNING

SOURCES

Answers in Genesis. Answers in Genesis is an Apologetics Ministry, www.answersingenesis.org.

Answers Research Journal. Answers in Genesis, Inc., www. answersresearchjournal.org.

Ballard, Robert, and Evan Lubofsky. The Discovery of Hydrothermal Vents. *Oceannus / Woods Hole Oceanographic Institution*, www.whoi.edu.

Behe, Michael. *AZQuotes*, www.azquotes.com/author/1143-Michael_Behe.

Behe, Michael. *Discovery Institute*, www.discovery.org/p/behe.

Behe, Michael. *Darwin's Black Box: The Biochemical Challenge to Evolution*. Free Press, 1996.

Biblical Science Institute. Dr. Jason Lisle, www.biblicalscienceinstitute.com.

Biblical Science Institute. Dr. Jason Lisle, biblicalscienceinstitute. com.

Buonarroti, Michelangelo. *AZQuotes*, www.azquotes.com/ author/10049-Michelangelo.

Cold-Case Christianity. J. Warner Wallace, www.coldcasechristianity.com.

CREATION.COM. Creation Ministries International, www. creation.com.

Crick, Francis. *AZQuotes*, www.azquotes.com/author/ 3404-Francis_Crick.

Darwin, Charles. *Origin of Species by Means of Natural Selection, or the Preservation of Favoured Races in the Struggle for Life*. Dover Thrift Editions Paperback first published: 1859, 2006.

Dawkins, Richard. *AZQuotes*, www.azquotes.com/ author/3748-Richard_Dawkins.

Dawkins, Richard. *The God Delusion*. Bantam Books, 2006.

120

Dembski, William A. *AZQuotes*, www.azquotes.com/
author/3855-William_A_Dembski?p=2.

Dembski, William A. Discovery Institute, www.discovery.org/p/
dembski.

Discovery Institute. www.discovery.org.

DISCOVERY SCIENCE. YouTube, uploaded by A Program of
Discovery Institute, 21 Oct. 2012, www.youtube.com/chan-
nel/UCm3i_fqq8dqsV-dTAriv2KA.

Edwards v. Aguillard. *Oyez*, www.oyez.org/cases/1986/85-1513.

Einstein, Albert. *AZQuotes*, www.azquotes.com/author/4399-Al-
bert_Einstein.

EN Evolution News. *Evolution News & Science Today*, www.
evolutionnews.org.

Epicurus. *AZQuotes*, www.azquotes.com/author/4529-Epicurus.

ESA Planck Mission. European Space Agency, www.esa.int/
Enabling_Support/Operations/Planck.

Faulkner, D. R. *Answers in Genesis*, Creation Ministries International, www.answersingenesis.org/bios/danny-faulkner.

Faulkner, Danny. *Thoughts on the Raq a and a Possible Explanation for the Cosmic Microwave Background.* Answers Research
Journal, 2016, pp. 57 65, www.answersresearchjournal.org/
raqia-cosmic-microwave-background.

Frost, Robert. *AZQuotes*, www.azquotes.com/author/5203-Rob-
ert_Frost.

Galilei, Galileo. *AZQuotes*, www.azquotes.com/
author/5284-Galileo_Galilei.

Gledhill, Linden. *Turns Out Crystallized DNA Is Crazy Pretty
Linden Gledhill Transforms Crystallized DNA into Beautiful Abstract Works of Art.* WIRED, Laura Mallonee/, www.
wired.com/2015/08/linden-gledhill-crystalized-dna.

Gohd, Chelsea. *Are Liquid Crystals Responsible for the Origins of
Life on Earth?* Discover, Kalmbach Media Co., 4 Oct. 2018,
www.discovermagazine.com.

Haeckel, Ernst. *AZQuotes*, www.azquotes.com/author/23428-Ernst_Haeckel.

Harris, Sam. *AZQuotes*, www.azquotes.com/author/6310-Sam_Harris.

Hawking, Stephen. *AZQuotes*, www.azquotes.com/author/6401-Stephen_Hawking.

Hitchens, Christopher. *AZQuotes*, www.azquotes.com/author/6756-Christopher_Hitchens.

Holmdel Horn Antenna. *Existing National Historic Landmarks for Astronomy*, National Park Service, www.nps.gov/parkhistory/online_books/butowsky5/astro4k.htm.

Howell, Elizabeth. *What Is the Big Bang Theory?* Space, www.space.com.

Hugo, Victor. *AZQuotes*, www.azquotes.com/author/7021-Victor_Hugo.

Huterer, Dragan. Cosmically Aligned. Cosmology Magazine, Dec. 2007, www.personal.umich.edu/~huterer/PRESS/CMB_Huterer.pdf.

Is Genesis History? The Documentary Film., www.isgenesishistory.com.

Jastrow, Robert. *AZQuotes*, www.azquotes.com/author/29579-Robert_Jastrow.

Journey. Music by the Band Journey, www.journeymusic.com.

Journey the Band, www.journeymusic.com.

Kaye, Danny. *AZQuotes*, www.azquotes.com/author/7795-Danny_Kaye.

King, Martin L. *Quote Investigator*, www.quoteinvestigator.com/2012/11/15/arc-of-universe.

King, Martin Luther, Jr. *AZQuotes*, www.azquotes.com/author/8044-Martin_Luther_King_Jr?p=7.

Kitzmiller v. Dover Area School District. Wikisource, wikisource.org/wiki/Kitzmiller_v._Dover_Area_School_District.

Krauss, Lawrence M. *AZQuotes*, www.azquotes.com/author/8264-Lawrence_M_Krauss?p=2.

Lemaitre, Georges. *AZQuotes*, www.azquotes.com/author/28144-Georges_Lemaitre.

Lennox. J. John Lennox, www.johnlennox.org.

Lennox, John. *AZQuotes*, www.azquotes.com/author/22896-John_Lennox.

Lewis, C. S. *The Official Website of C. S. Lewis*, www.cslewis.com/us.

Lubofsky, Evan. *The Discovery of Hydrothermal Vents*. Oceanus, Woods Hole Oceanographic Institution, 11 June 2018, www.whoi.edu.

Marley, B. Bad Boys Lyrics. LyricsFreak, www.lyricsfreak.com/b/bob+marley/bad+boys_20644274.html.

McDowell, S. *Sean McDowell*, www.seanmcdowell.org.

Meyer, S. C. *Darwin's Doubt: The Explosive Origin of Animal Life and the Case for Intelligent Design*. HarperCollins Publishers, 2013.

Meyer, S. C. *Signature in the Cell DNA and the Evidence for Intelligent Design*. HarperOne, 2009.

Meyer, S.C. *Signature in the Cell: Stephen Meyer Faces His Critics*, Pt. 1: The Presentation. YouTube, uploaded by Discovery Institute, 14 Feb. 2014, www.youtube.com/watch?v=eW6e-gHV6jAw.

Meyer, Stephen C. *AZQuotes*, www.azquotes.com/author/42197-Stephen_C_Meyer.

Meyer, Stephen C. Discovery Institute, www.discovery.org/p/meyer.

Newton, Isaac. *AZQuotes*, www.azquotes.com/author/10784-Isaac_Newton.

Penzias, Arno A. *The Nobel Prize*, The Nobel Prize in Physics 1978, www.nobelprize.org/prizes/physics/1978/penzias/facts.

Picasso, Pablo. *AZQuotes*, www.azquotes.com/author/11640-Pablo_Picasso.

Plack Satellite UK Outreach Site. European Space Agency, plancksatellite.org.uk.

Planck, Max. *AZQuotes*, www.azquotes.com/author/11714-Max_Planck.

Pollock, Jackson. *AZQuotes*, www.azquotes.com/author/11762-Jackson_Pollock.

The Principle Movie. YouTube, uploaded by Robert Sungenis, 6 Dec. 2013, www.youtube.com/channel/UCwyM0CLy-wu127gMw7aLC0TA.

Roosevelt, Eleanor. *AZQuotes*, www.azquotes.com/author/12603-Eleanor_Roosevelt.

Sagan, Carl. *AZQuotes*, www.azquotes.com/author/12883-Carl_Sagan.

Shakespeare, W. Sonnet 60. *The Society of Classical Poets*, www.classicalpoets.org/2018/04/08/10-greatest-shakespeare-sonnets-an-immortal-series.

Sky Scholar. *YouTube,* uploaded by Pierre-Marie Robitaille, 21 May 2020, www.youtube.com/watch?v=EtHVDzff6LM.

Stein, Ben. *Expelled: No Intelligence Allowed*. YouTube, uploaded by Maxavail, 14 June 2012, www.youtube.com/watch?v=V5EPymcWp-g.

Strickland, Lloyd. Why Is There Something Rather than Nothing? *The Conversation*, www.theconversation.com/answering-the-biggest-question-of-all-why-is-there-something-rather-than-nothing-65865.

Sutter, Paul M. The Axis of Evil. *YouTube*, uploaded by Ask a Spaceman, 25 May 2017, www.youtube.com/watch?v=hjVC-jdX5XRw.

Tolkien, J. R. R. *AZQuotes*, www.azquotes.com/author/14701-J_R_R_Tolkien.

Trilobite Fossil. *Britannica*, www.britannica.com/animal/trilobite.

The Truth Source Revealing Relevant Political and Religious News, History, Topics and Truths. *The Truth Source*, www.thetruthsource.org/creation-vs-evolution-debate-part-iv.

Uber. *Uber Technologies*, Inc, www.uber.com.

Watson, James D. *AZQuotes*, www.azquotes.com/author/15351-James_D_Watson.

The Wilkinson Microwave Anisotropy Probe (WMAP). *National Aeronautics and Space Administration*, map.gsfc.nasa.gov.

Williams, T. *A Streetcar Named Desire*. New American Library, 1947.

Wilson, Robert W. The Nobel Prize in Physics 1978. *The Nobel Prize*, www.nobelprize.org/prizes/physics/1978/wilson/facts.

BIBLICAL SOURCES

King James Version (KJV), New King James Version (NKJV), English Standard Version (ESV), New International Version (NIV), New American Standard Bible (NASB), Berean Literal Bible (BLB).

ABOUT THE AUTHOR

Joseph Paquette was born and raised in Rhode Island, an only child of Joseph Sr. and Angelena (Angie) Paquette. Back in the day, within their neighborhood, his extended family on both sides was so extensive that if Joseph randomly threw a baseball into the air, it would undoubtedly be caught by a cousin. And back in the day, he threw many baseballs. Joseph is a visual artist and playwright. To support his passions of painting and writing, he's worked as an art instructor, national park ranger, land surveyor, and draftsman. His plays have been performed in Rhode Island and New York City, with other works published by Smith & Kraus Publishers. But, more importantly, he has two grandsons, Nathan and Zachary, who entertain, inspire, and also throw a lot of baseballs.

For production and performance rights of the play, *Axis of Beginning*, you may contact Joseph at: axisofbeginning@gmail.com.

www.ingramcontent.com/pod-product-compliance
Lightning Source LLC
LaVergne TN
LVHW021349080426
835508LV00020B/2179